STECK-VAUGHN

PORTRAIT OF AMERICA

Kansas

OK MB ME BL DF LM BP

Steck-Vaughn Company

Executive Editor	Diane Sharpe
Senior Editor	Martin S. Saiewitz
Design Manager	Pamela Heaney
Photo Editor	Margie Foster

Proof Positive/Farrowlyne Associates, Inc.
Program Editorial, Revision Development, Design, and Production

Consultant: Loretta D. Hiner, Management Analyst, Department of Commerce and Housing

Published by Raintree Steck-Vaughn Publishers, an imprint of Steck-Vaughn Company.

A Turner Educational Services, Inc. book. Based on the Portrait of America television series by R. E. (Ted) Turner.

Cover Photo: Wheat field and barn by © Bryan Peterson / The Stock Market

Library of Congress Cataloging-in-Publication Data

Thompson, Kathleen.
    Kansas / Kathleen Thompson.
        p.   cm. — (Portrait of America)
    "A Turner book."
    "Based on the Portrait of America television series"—T.p. verso.
    Includes index.
    ISBN 0-8114-7336-8 (library binding).—ISBN 0-8114-7441-0 (softcover)
    1. Kansas—Juvenile literature. [1. Kansas.] I. Title.
    II. Series: Thompson, Kathleen. Portrait of America.
    F681.3.T48   1996
    978.1—dc20   95-42907
                                                         CIP
                                                          AC

Printed and Bound in the United States of America

1 2 3 4 5 6 7 8 9 10 WZ 98 97 96 95

Acknowledgments
The publishers wish to thank the following for permission to reproduce photographs:
P. 7 © Andy Sacks/Tony Stone Images; p. 8 © Renee Lynn/Tony Stone Images; p. 10 © Michael Reagan; p. 13 (both), 14, 15, 16 Kansas State Historical Society, Topeka; p. 18 (top) Kansas State Historical Society, Topeka, (bottom) U.S. Senate Photo; p. 19 U.S. Senate Photo; p. 20 Boot Hill Museum, Dodge City, Kansas; p. 21 (both) Kansas State Historical Society, Topeka; p. 22 © John Schlageck/Kansas Farm Bureau; p. 24 (top) © Michael Reagan, (bottom) © John Schlageck/Kansas Farm Bureau; p. 25 (top, bottom) © Michael Reagan, (center) Gates Learjet; p. 26 (top) Kansas Wheat Commission, (bottom) © Michael Reagan; p. 27 (both) Kansas Travel & Tourism; p. 28 Kansas State Historical Society, Topeka; pp. 29, 30 © Michael Reagan; p. 31 (top) Kansas Travel & Tourism, (bottom) © Michael Reagan; p. 32 © Superstock; p. 34 AP/Wide World; p. 35 Kansas State Historical Society, Topeka; p. 36 (top) Kansas Travel & Tourism, (bottom) U.S. Army Photograph, Fort Leavenworth, Kansas; p. 37 (top) Institute of Jazz, Rutgers University, (bottom) Kansas Travel & Tourism; p. 38 © Michael Reagan; p. 39 © D. Dancer; p. 40 Gordon Parks/Life Magazine © Time Warner, Inc.; p. 41 AP/Wide World; p. 42 Kansas Travel & Tourism; p. 44 John Schlageck/Kansas Farm Bureau; p. 46 One Mile Up; p. 47 (left) One Mile Up, (center, right) Kansas Travel & Tourism.

STECK-VAUGHN

PORTRAIT OF AMERICA

Kansas

Kathleen Thompson

A Turner Book

RSVP

RAINTREE
STECK-VAUGHN
PUBLISHERS
The Steck-Vaughn Company

Austin, Texas

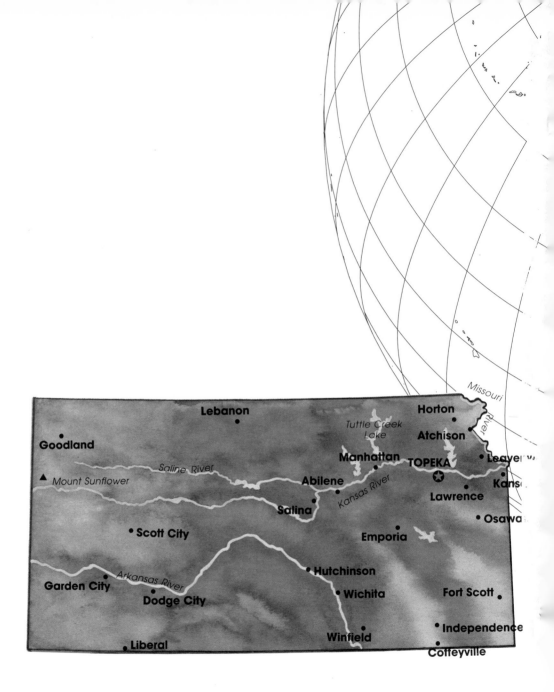

Kansas

Lebanon
Goodland
Mount Sunflower
Saline River
Abilene
Salina
Scott City
Garden City
Arkansas River
Dodge City
Liberal

Tuttle Creek Lake
Manhattan
Kansas River
Hutchinson
Wichita
Emporia
Winfield

Horton
Atchison
TOPEKA
Leavenworth
Lawrence
Kansas City
Osawatomie
Fort Scott
Independence
Coffeyville

Missouri River

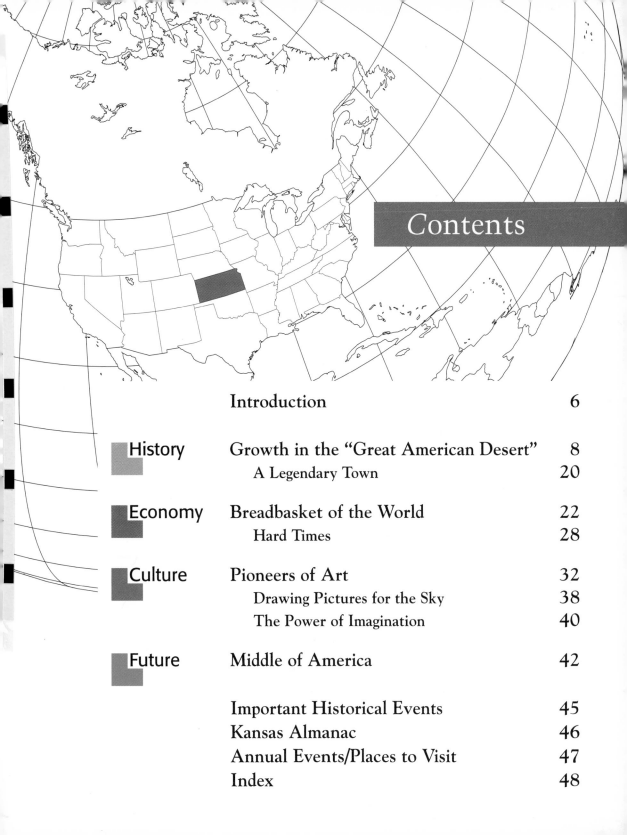

Contents

Introduction

The landscape of Kansas has not changed much over the years. The wide open skies and unbroken horizon familiar to the early settlers are still part of its beauty. Its people still follow time-tested methods of getting things done. Early settlers hitched their horses to plows and grew row upon row of wheat. Now tractors do the job of horses, but Kansas is still known as the nation's breadbasket. Its vast wheat crop has fed much of the world for over a century. Perhaps because the state provides food for our tables, Kansas feels like home. The familiar strains of "Home on the Range" call us back to the heartland of America. Kansas is what America thinks of as the bountiful, quiet beauty of home.

Kansas is a leading agricultural state. It has more than thirty million acres of cropland in production.

Kansas

rms, cattle, Great Plains

Growth in the "Great American Desert"

The earliest known civilization in the area of Kansas was that of the Paleo-Indians. These people hunted mammoths and other prehistoric beasts as early as 13,000 B.C. Later, they grew their own food and lived in villages.

By about A.D. 1000, the Paleo-Indians had split up into several groups. Among these were the Wichita, the Kansa, the Osage, and the Pawnee. The Wichita lived in huts made of grass. The other groups built houses from mud or clay. Like their ancestors, these Native Americans lived by farming and hunting.

Later the Kiowa, the Cheyenne, the Comanche, and the Arapaho came to present-day Kansas. These groups arrived on horses, a method unknown to the Native Americans already living in the area. European explorers were responsible for bringing horses to the North American continent in the sixteenth century. The Native Americans on horseback probably had met the Spanish who were exploring areas of the South and the Southwest.

Hundreds of years ago, sixty million buffalo lived in the Great Plains region. Today, there are less than four hundred buffalo left in Kansas.

The red clay hills on the Kansas prairies don't look much different today than they did to the early explorers.

Spanish explorer Francisco Vásquez de Coronado of Spain set out in 1541 to search for the so-called Seven Cities of Cíbola. These legendary cities were supposed to be made of gold. Coronado gave up his search when he reached the center of what is now Kansas. He spent some time with the Wichita people before he returned home empty-handed.

In 1682 explorer René-Robert Cavelier, Sieur de La Salle, claimed a large part of North America, including Kansas, for France. A few settlers, mostly fur trappers, arrived from France. The settlers eventually built military and trading posts in the northeastern part of the state. By 1744 they were carrying on a profitable fur trading business with the Native Americans.

In 1803 President Thomas Jefferson made a deal with French Emperor Napoleon Bonaparte. Napoleon offered to sell all of France's claims in North America. The deal became known as the Louisiana Purchase. France's claims extended from Louisiana to the Canadian border and from the Mississippi River to the Rocky Mountains. This area, called the Louisiana Territory, included much of present-day Kansas.

The next year, Meriwether Lewis and William Clark were sent by President Jefferson to explore the Louisiana Territory. They explored the eastern edge of Kansas along the Missouri River before moving on. In 1806 Zebulon Pike explored the area and judged it unlivable. When Pike drew up maps of his explorations, he marked the Kansas area as the "Great American Desert." About 15 years later, Major Stephen H. Long and his group explored the eastern border. Long agreed with Pike's opinion.

The government decided that since settlers wouldn't want the land, they could move Native Americans there. Beginning in 1830 the government forced about thirty Native American groups to move to Kansas. These groups included the Chippewa, Delaware, Fox, Iowa, Kickapoo, Pottawatomie, Ottawa, Shawnee, and Wyandot. For most of these

Spaniards led by Francisco Vásquez de Coronado came to Kansas in search of the Seven Cities of Cíbola.

groups, the climate and land in Kansas did not fit their established way of life. They did not know how to clothe, feed, and house themselves in this strange place. Most groups lost about half of their people either during the journey or in trying to adapt to this harsh new land.

In 1854 Congress passed the Kansas-Nebraska Act, which set up a territorial government in what is now Kansas and Nebraska. The United States government wanted to develop the economy of the territory. One way of doing this was to build a railway through this area from Chicago to the Pacific Ocean.

The Kansas-Nebraska Act stirred up the slavery issue. The Missouri Compromise of 1820 had already established the law regarding which new states could allow slaves. The compromise said that no territory north of the southern border of Missouri, except Missouri itself, could enter the Union as a slave state. But the Kansas-Nebraska Act changed that. It said that each territory could decide for itself whether or not to allow slavery.

The Kansas Territory soon became a battleground for the slavery issue. Both proslavery forces and abolitionists, people who were against slavery, began moving to Kansas. Each was trying to populate the territory with people from their side of the argument. Many violent clashes broke out near the border between Kansas and proslavery Missouri. Missouri men called "Border Ruffians" regularly crossed into Kansas and attacked abolitionists. Fighting became so fierce that the territory was called "Bleeding Kansas."

The town of Lawrence was sacked by Border Ruffians in 1856. This drawing shows the wreckage of the Free State Hotel.

The election to decide whether Kansas would allow slaves or not was held in 1855. Armed Missourians forced their way into Kansas voting places and voted illegally. The number of votes was about twice the actual population of Kansas. The proslavery voters won. The new proslavery government started passing laws right away. Among other things, these new laws stated that anyone who helped to free a slave could be sentenced to death.

In May 1856, proslavery forces destroyed part of the town of Lawrence. Some of its residents were killed. But the antislavery forces fought back. A group led by the abolitionist John Brown killed five proslavery men. Even more riots followed. About two hundred people were killed in Bleeding Kansas from 1854 to 1861.

Kansas at last gained statehood in January 1861 as a free state. But the Union that it joined was falling apart. The Civil War began in April of that same year. The Southern states had withdrawn to form a

Kansas abolitionist John Brown was hanged in Virginia for leading a slave revolt at Harpers Ferry (now in West Virginia) in 1859.

Confederacy that allowed slavery. But President Abraham Lincoln vowed to bring the Union back together. Almost twenty thousand Kansans fought for the Union. This number was about two thirds of the number of adult men in the entire state. No other state sent such a large percentage of its population.

One of the few Civil War battles that took place in Kansas was also one of the most brutal. In 1863 Lawrence was again attacked, this time by a group led by the rebellious Confederate soldier named William Quantrill. The town was burned, and nearly 150 Kansans, mostly people who were not soldiers, were killed.

After the Civil War, many settlers came to Kansas. This was partly because of the Homestead Act of 1862. This act promised 160 acres of land for only ten dollars to any settler who was the head of a household. In return, the settlers, called homesteaders, had to promise to farm and develop the land for five years.

Railroads brought even more people. The Kansas Pacific Railroad reached Abilene in 1867. The town became the most convenient place from which to ship Texas cattle to the East. Texas cowboys started driving huge herds of longhorn cattle up to Abilene. Over thirty thousand cattle passed through in Abilene's first year as a "cow town." As the railroads reached farther west, more Kansas cow towns, such as Dodge City and Wichita, sprang up. These towns earned a reputation for lawlessness. Legendary sheriffs such as Wyatt Earp, Wild Bill Hickok, and Bat Masterson kept the peace. The cross-country railroads reached Texas by the end

Raiding officers such as William Quantrill were often not acting under orders from their Confederate leaders. Such ruthless rebel soldiers came to be called "bushwhackers."

of the century. When that happened, there was no longer any need for cowboys to drive the cattle to the railroads in the Kansas cow towns.

The same year that the railroad reached Abilene, the United States government made a treaty with the Native Americans in the Midwest. The government promised to help them resettle in Oklahoma. Many Native American groups left their homes for the food, money, and clothing the government said it would provide in Oklahoma. Few of the government's promises were kept, however. When the Native Americans tried to return to Kansas, settlers had taken over their former lands. The Native Americans were enraged at this betrayal, so for the next ten years, they led raids on the settlers. Then in 1878, exhausted and outnumbered, the last of these Native American

Many pioneer families passed through Kansas following the Oregon Trail, which stretched from Missouri to Oregon. Covered wagons like the one shown were called Conestogas.

groups had no choice but to return to Oklahoma and try to resettle once again.

Settlers continued to arrive in Kansas, including Swedes, Germans, and African Americans. These new residents of western Kansas and other parts of the Great Plains were called "sodbusters." This was because they plowed the dense prairie earth, the sod, to start their farms. Because wood was scarce, many of them even made houses out of blocks of sod.

Life was difficult for the farmers in Kansas. Not many crops grew well in prairie soil. What's more, the weather was severe, and water was scarce. Then in 1874 a religious group from Russia called the Mennonites brought a kind of wheat to Kansas that could survive harsh winters. It was called Turkey Red wheat, and the conditions in Kansas were perfect for it. The wheat flourished all over the state. Eventually Kansas and the other Plains states were producing more wheat than Americans could consume. Kansas was called the "Breadbasket of the World," a nickname the state still carries today.

In 1887 the first woman mayor in the United States, Susanna Salter, took office in Argonia, Kansas. At about the same time, women were given the right to own land and to vote in certain elections.

In the late 1880s, farmers and ranchers formed a group called the Farmers' Alliance to try to influence government policy. Members of the Farmers' Alliance joined a political party called the Populist party. The Populists elected many state officials, including a United States senator in 1890.

The Populists had a very good influence on Kansas politics. They passed laws to make telegraph services, banks, railroads, and other companies run more fairly. Populists also helped to make voting an easier process with less corruption.

The Populist party declined in the late 1890s, but its success paved the way for reforms and changes made by many other groups in Kansas. By 1912, Kansas women had the right to vote in all elections. Labor parties also flourished after the Populists. Kansas was one of the first states to pass a law limiting work days to eight hours. It was also one of the first to restrict child labor.

In the first part of this century, Kansas was booming. The United States was exporting wheat overseas. World War I brought additional demand for wheat. It soon became the state's number one crop. Agricultural technology helped Kansas produce a better crop with every new season.

But the high wheat demand persuaded farmers to find more places to grow crops. Trees were cut down to

This tractor in Dodge City was completely covered by drifting dust during the Dust Bowl years of the 1930s.

In 1978 Nancy Landon Kassebaum was elected and became the first woman United States senator from Kansas.

make room for fields. When especially dry conditions occurred in the 1930s, there were no trees to block the strong prairie winds from blowing away the dry soil. The land became like a desert. Nothing would grow. Farms failed, and many people left to try to find work in other states. Western Kansas and the other Plains states became known as the Dust Bowl.

The 1930s were also the time of the Great Depression. Millions of people all over the country were unemployed. The economy was at a standstill. It was a hard time for the country. But it was even harder for the Plains people, who watched as their land was destroyed by winds and drought.

After the 1930s, improved farming techniques and increased use of irrigation improved the farming situation greatly. World War II brought back demand for Kansas wheat. Kansas oil, natural gas, and helium were also in demand. Kansas began building airplanes for the military buildup that accompanied World War II. General Dwight D. Eisenhower, commander of the Allied forces during World War II, was from Kansas. Eisenhower was elected President in 1952.

In the 1950s many Kansans found that the struggles over the rights of African Americans hadn't ended with the Civil War, almost a century earlier. As in many other states across the nation, African Americans in Kansas were not treated as full American citizens. When 11-year-old Linda Brown was not allowed into an all-white school in Topeka, her father sued the town's Board of Education. The case went to the United States Supreme Court in 1954. *Brown v. Board of Education of Topeka, Kansas* was a landmark decision against the separation of races. The Supreme Court ruled that preventing Linda Brown from attending the school was unconstitutional. The law demanded that schools across the nation open their doors to people of all races.

An economic slump in the early 1980s hurt the state's farm owners, and many of them left farming for good. But the state no longer depends entirely on its farms. New industries and new people have come into the state. The population has increased steadily for the past forty years. Kansans believe that their state possesses what many Americans value today: smaller urban centers, clean air, and an emphasis on self-reliance. The area that explorers once called the "Great American Desert" now has a strong reputation for good government and progressive education. That reputation is the seed for growth in the new century.

United States Senator Robert Dole was first elected to that office in 1968. Since then he has become nationally known as Senate majority leader, Senate minority leader, national chairman of the Republican party, and candidate for President.

19

A Legendary Town

Most people have seen movies or read books about the Old West. The cowboys and the towns they rode into are legendary. This means that the truth about the West is often exaggerated. Dodge City has become a symbol of the Western legend—a place of gamblers, rustlers, and ranchers.

Dodge City was founded in 1871 on a vast prairie that was the home of the Comanche and the Kiowa. At that time the railroad had not yet been built through Kansas. The land was home to some families of settlers and an estimated five to eight million buffalo. When some businessmen saw that the Santa Fe Railroad was being built near Fort Dodge, they thought it would be a good idea to build a town near the tracks. The town would give the settlers a place to shop, and it would give buffalo hunters a place to relax. It also gave the soldiers a place to get away from the fort.

By the 1880s Dodge City was a boom town. Cowboys drove longhorn cattle north along the Western Trail to Dodge City. The cattle were then shipped by railroad to St. Louis and other cities. The city's peak year was in 1884, when over eight hundred million head of cattle passed through.

Dodge City's famous lawmen—Wyatt Earp, Bat Masterson, and Doc Holliday—are Western legends. They are portrayed as fair but trigger-happy men trying to bring law and order to

This scene of Dodge City's Front Street may look innocent, but the town was once called the "Wickedest Little City in America."

the town. In truth, however, neither Bat Masterson nor Doc Holliday ever killed anyone in Dodge. As sheriff of Dodge City, Wyatt Earp's job was to keep the peace. His job also included fixing the streets and the sidewalks. Making the streets safe sometimes meant arresting people. Other times it meant filling potholes.

Gunfights, although not always deadly, were common in Dodge City as well. When gunfighters or cowboys were killed, they were buried at Boot Hill Cemetery. This place got its name because the men were laid to rest with their boots on.

Before Dodge City became a cow town, it was a buffalo town. From 1872 to 1874, 850,000 buffalo hides were shipped out of Dodge City. By 1875 there weren't enough buffalo left to hunt.

If you visit Dodge City today, you'll get some idea of what life was like there during the late 1800s. Front Street, once the city's main street, has been completely reconstructed. So has Boot Hill Cemetery. In fact, the famous cemetery now has its own museum. There you can see a video presentation about the history of Dodge City. In the summer there are daily stagecoach rides. You might even see stunt performers in a very real-looking gunfight. The legendary town of Dodge City is still in Kansas. The people there take pleasure in presenting the best of the Old West.

Bartholomew "Bat" Masterson was sheriff of Ford County, where Dodge City is located, from 1878 to 1880.

Breadbasket of the World

In spring they ripple like a sweet green sea in the constant wind. In summer they roll like a golden ocean. They are the wheat fields of Kansas, a living symbol of the United States. Wheat is what gave the Kansas economy its start. Today, there are wheat fields in every one of the state's 105 counties. Kansas still leads the nation in wheat production. In fact, only seven countries in the world grow more wheat than the state of Kansas does. It isn't likely that Kansas will have to give up its nickname "Breadbasket of the World" any time soon.

As important as wheat is to Kansas, it isn't the only grain harvested in the state. Many of the nation's farm animals rely on Kansas and its abundant fields of grain sorghum, which is made into livestock feed. Now farming makes up only about four percent of Kansas' gross state product, which is the value of goods and services produced in Kansas in a year. Other crops grown in the state include corn and soybeans in

Kansas is known as the Wheat State because it produces more wheat than any other state in the country. There is not a county in Kansas where wheat is not grown.

above. This photo shows a row of towering grain-storage elevators.

below. Grain sorghum is an ideal Kansas crop because it is resistant to drought and heat.

eastern Kansas and irrigated crops of various types in the western half of the state.

Not all of the people employed on farms work in the fields. Many people work on cattle ranches and dairy farms. These days beef cattle are the state's most valuable farm product—even more important than wheat. Beef cattle are responsible for about fifty percent of Kansas' farm income. Cow towns may have faded from the Kansas map, but the cows themselves never left. Only Texas raises more cattle than Kansas. Kansas farmers also raise hogs, sheep, and chickens.

Manufacturing is also a major contributor to Kansas' economy. Transportation equipment—especially the aviation industry—is Kansas' most important area of manufacturing. Kansas ranks number one in the world in general aviation aircraft. The state also manufactures military aircraft, missiles, and aircraft parts. Transportation manufacturers also make railroad cars, mobile homes, snowplows, automobiles, trailers, and tires.

You might expect a state with so many farms to be involved in food processing, too. Kansas processes the harvested wheat into flour, taking the wheat one step closer to the breadbasket. Kansas mills produce more flour than any other state. Meat packing and processing plants are also an important part of Kansas' food-processing industry.

Mining has been a significant part of the Kansas economy ever since the first commercially successful oil well was drilled in Neodsha in 1892. Petroleum production is still the leading mining activity in the

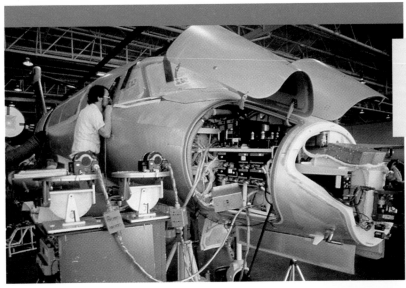

The aircraft industry has helped to place Kansas tenth in the nation in the number of high-tech industries.

state. Natural gas is also an important mining product, as are salt, limestone, coal, and helium. Most of the electrical power sold in Kansas annually is generated by its own coal- and gas-fired power plants. Several of Kansas' claims to fame are mining related—the state has a salt deposit and a natural gas field that are

This business jet is built by Learjet in Wichita.

These aircraft workers are part of the 16 percent of Kansas' workforce that is employed in manufacturing.

To make flour, the kernel of the wheat is ground. To prepare white flour, mills remove bran and wheat germ from the kernel. Unfortunately, bran and wheat germ are the most nutritious parts of wheat.

This man is working on an oil-drilling rig in Kansas.

among the largest in the world. Although mining produces only about two percent of Kansas' gross state product, almost every county mines a natural resource.

In recent years, service industries have come to dominate Kansas' economy, as they have in most of the other states. Service industries are those in which people don't manufacture an actual product. Instead, they may work at a department store, a bank, or an insurance company. The state's service industries create over seventy percent of its gross state product.

You may be surprised to find out that one of Kansas' fastest-growing service industries is travel and tourism. Tourism raises almost $2.5 billion for the state each year. Tourism-related industries are Kansas' fifth-largest employer. The United States Department of Commerce recently said that in the early 1990s, Kansas' international tourism increased faster than any other state's.

This means that more tourists from foreign countries are visiting Kansas than ever before.

More and more Kansans are seeing the rest of the world, too. The state's economic leaders have been traveling the world to increase international trade with the state. London, Mexico, and Japan have recently welcomed Kansas trade talks. In 1993 the Leningrad region of Russia signed a trade agreement with Kansas. The agreement encourages not only exports and imports but cultural exchanges as well.

It is this kind of wide-reaching vision and economic flexibility that has made Kansas one of the nation's most economically stable states. Thanks to its many and varied industries, it should remain strong for years to come.

At Harrod's in London, a whole booth is devoted to Kansas tourist information.

Wichita, the state's largest city, is one of Kansas' two most productive areas for wholesale and retail trade.

Hard Times

Things are getting harder and harder for family farms across the nation. Just because Kansas farmers work in the state called the "Breadbasket of the World," they're not any exception to these hard times. Arthur Sayler has seen a lot of ups and downs in his years as a farmer in Kansas. He even farmed back in the 1930s when years without rain turned Kansas into a nightmare of dust. "It just looked like a cloud," he remembers. "It was black. It was solid dirt. Everybody'd go in the house. And you couldn't even see the porch post. It really was terrible."

The long drought and the dust destroyed many Kansas farms. Farmers had to leave and find work elsewhere. Times have not been quite as hard since. But today's farmers still do not have an easy life. Many farms are failing. To succeed as a farmer takes all you have—and sometimes more.

Tom Giessel has been farming in Kansas all his life. "You have to push yourself to the absolute limits," he

The farmer in this photo is shoveling dust out of his fields. The dust storms of the 1930s carried the topsoil off fifty million acres of land.

Arthur Sayler lived through one of the worst environmental disasters in history, the dust storms of the 1930s.

says. "And you cannot make a wrong turn. You can't plant the wrong direction. You can't sell the wrong day. You do any one of these things, any little thing wrong, and you're out."

Running a farm is a full-time job for everyone in the Giessel family. Tom's wife, Sheryl, wasn't raised on a farm, but her marriage has taught her the hardships of the farming life. "Well, it's sort of like having two marriages," she says. "One to your husband and the commitment that's involved there, and one to the farm. Because there are just certain times of the year that the farm and its demands are going to come first."

The harvest is one of those times. When the farm family goes out into the field for harvest, their whole year's work—and sometimes their whole farm—is at stake. As Tom says, "The

Tom and Sheryl Giessel are pictured here with one of their three children. Between farming and family life, the Giessels work double time.

harvest is the culmination of everything. It's a matter of do or die. So you hope that equipment holds together. You hope your emotions hold together, and then hope your family holds together because you need everybody you've got for every minute of every day."

Sheryl helps out a lot on the farm. During harvest time she fills the towering grain bins and runs the baler, the machine that binds hay into bundles called bales. But Sheryl's help still isn't enough. There is so much work during harvest time that the Giessels have to hire help in the months of October and November. Luckily, they can pay for such help and still keep their farm going. But it's not easy.

"Things are getting harder and harder all the time," says Sheryl. "There's less and less return on what we produce—our crops, cattle, hay." Many of the Giessels' neighbors have to hold down full-time jobs in addition to running their farms. And many of them have simply had to give up and leave.

The Giessels' farm has been handed down over many generations. But although they have three children, Tom and Sheryl may be the last generation of Giessels in farming. The farm is important to them, but their children's welfare is much more important. Tom and Sheryl want their children to be successful, however the chances of

This machine called a combine cuts and threshes wheat and other grains for harvest.

finding success in farming are becoming slimmer.

Arthur Sayler hopes that he can use his experience to help younger farmers like the Giessels find ways to make it through these hard times. "I've said a lot of times, 'If there's gonna get terrible hard times, I hope it's while some of us old boys are alive that went through the Depression.' I think it needs some of us around because, you know, reading some things . . . that's not as good as having somebody tell you." Hopefully, with everyone pulling together to help, things will improve for Kansas family farmers once again.

A combine harvests the kernel of wheat, but the rest of the plant is not wasted. The stems are dried to make straw.

Pioneers of Art

Kansas has quite an exciting pioneer history. In some ways, the pioneer spirit has been kept alive in Kansas' writers, musicians, actors, and artists.

Emmett Kelly was literally the most colorful of Kansas' famous natives—he was a clown. Born in Kansas, he spent his life traveling with circuses, including Ringling Brothers and Barnum and Bailey. America knew him as "Weary Willie," a sad-faced, shabby, but endearing hobo. Kelly was a pioneer of the sad clown character in America's circuses. Many clowns today use his Weary Willie as a model.

Charlie "Bird" Parker was a musical pioneer from Kansas. Born in Kansas City, this saxophonist, composer, and bandleader helped develop a style of jazz music called "bebop." This upbeat new sound became popular in the 1940s and influenced jazz music.

Another pioneer from Kansas was William Inge. He was one of the first playwrights to consider life in the Midwest a worthwhile subject for the stage. In 1953 he won the Pulitzer Prize for his play *Picnic*,

Kansans began building their state capitol in Topeka in 1866. They finished it 37 years later at a total cost of $3.2 million.

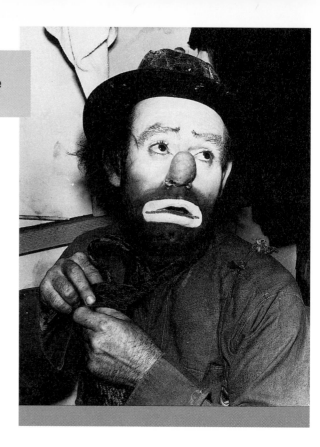

which takes place in his hometown of Independence. Soon, audiences across the nation knew about the town's annual celebration called Neewollah—which is *Halloween* spelled backwards! Like a true pioneer, Inge tried his hand at other types of writing, too. For example, his screenwriting won him an Academy Award for the 1961 film *Splendor in the Grass*. Like Inge's plays, this film script was about life in the Midwest.

Poet and novelist Edgar Lee Masters, born in Garnett, also wrote about life in the small towns of the Midwest. His most famous work was a group of poems called *Spoon River Anthology*, published in 1915. Each poem is narrated by a small-town Midwesterner after his or her death. The narrators relate the hardships and frustrations of life in a small town.

Another small-town Kansan writer was William Allen White. White was best known for his editorials in his hometown paper, the *Emporia Gazette*. In the early part of the twentieth century, people across the nation, not just in Kansas, read his insightful, fair-minded editorials. White won two Pulitzer Prizes, the first in 1922 for an editorial, and the second for his autobiography, published after his death.

Poet Gwendolyn Brooks is another Pulitzer Prize winner from Kansas. In fact in 1950, for her collection *Annie Allen*, she became the first African American poet to win the Pulitzer. Most of her poems are about her childhood in Chicago, and she was appointed Poet Laureate of Illinois in 1969. But she was born in Topeka, and proud residents won't let you forget it.

But the culture of Kansas isn't only about its people. The landscape of Kansas, crossed with history, has a powerful cultural influence. Historical sites include various forts and stations along the Santa Fe and Oregon trails and on the Pony Express route. The John Brown Memorial Park in Osawatomie contains the log cabin where the abolitionist John Brown lived. Many museums also celebrate this rich history. The largest in the state is the Kansas Museum of History in Topeka, which is actually located on a branch of the pioneers' Oregon Trail.

Because Kansas lacks cities of great size, many cultural activities are concentrated in the universities. For example, the University of Kansas has an excellent

William A. White brought the Midwest to the nation with his editorials written in the early 1900s.

These people are riding in a covered wagon, or Conestoga, at Bull Whacker Days. Every year the people of Olathe commemorate the bull whackers who drove cattle over the Santa Fe and Oregon trails.

Established in 1827, Fort Leavenworth is the oldest active Army post west of the Mississippi River. Today, Fort Leavenworth is the home of the United States Army Command, General Staff College, and Leavenworth Prison.

museum of natural history and an art museum. The Mulvane Art Center of Washburn University in Topeka is another example.

Kansas also has a number of unique historical museums. The Antique Doll Museum in Abilene is one of the few doll museums in the United States. Many of the dolls in this collection date as far back as the mid-1800s. The U.S. Cavalry Museum in Junction City chronicles the colorful history of the American horse soldier. Among the museum's collection are original art by Frederic Remington, authentic cavalry uniforms, and weapons equipment.

The Kansas Arts Commission has been formed to encourage development of the arts. The money is offered to communities and organizations that wish to develop cultural events. But much of Kansas' culture will probably always remain rooted in its rich, colorful history.

Born in Kansas City, Charlie Parker went on to become one of the greatest jazz musicians in music history.

Tourists in Liberal can visit Dorothy's house, the actual building used in filming the 1939 movie *The Wizard of Oz*. The house is located at 567 Yellowbrick Road.

Drawing Pictures for the Sky

Stan Herd, like many Kansans, grew up on a farm. Everyone thought Stan would become a farmer, too. But when he first learned to drive a tractor at age 12, he saw things a little bit differently than the rest of his family. He recalls, "I have always had a sense, I think, as a young man on a tractor, of the feeling of what it might look like from the air. The fact that I was on the earth and the birds flying over would look down and see me and see this strip of land I'm laying."

After Stan Herd graduated from high school, he left the farm to study art at Wichita State University. Remembering how he felt driving that tractor in his youth, he got an idea. What would happen if he used the tractor as a paintbrush, and a field as a canvas?

After five years, he at last found a farmer willing to sacrifice about 150 acres. Stan next had to find a tractor, seeds, and fuel. Then he calculated distances and measured the lay of the land with complicated instruments to make sure that he planted the seeds in the right spots. He carefully placed numbered markers in the field, then

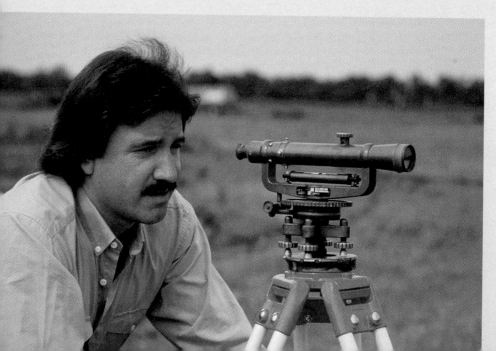

Stan Herd uses this instrument, called a transit, to measure the angles of his crop paintings.

This twenty-acre work, called "Sunflower Still Life," was made from alfalfa, soybeans, and sunflowers, all of which were harvested.

followed the markers on his tractor. After all that work, he still had to sit back and wait for the seeds to grow.

Rain poured down for three weeks on Stan's first project. When it finally stopped, even more wheat grew than he had planted. And the extra wheat came out the wrong color. He had to plow the whole picture again.

Stan now has the experience of 14 years of crop painting under his belt. "When I did my first field work I got the feeling that a lot of people considered it on the level of trying to get fifteen people into a phone booth. You know, this was another *Guinness Book of World Records* giant, fantastic thing. And it was a very serious thing for me. It was a very serious art form."

Now Stan Herd is not the only one who takes his "paintings" seriously. He gets support from the farmers of the area, people he has known all his life. The farmers believe in Stan Herd and his art. And many other people are beginning to believe in him, too. He completed a work in New York City, on an acre of land yet to be developed. More people than ever can see this one-acre landscape called *Countryside*. That is because in New York, they can view it from hills and high rises. In flat, undeveloped Kansas, anyone who wanted to see Stan's work had to rent a plane.

Like any artist, Stan is happy that more people are beginning to appreciate his work. But he also hopes that his art will help revive people's respect for the land.

The Power of Imagination

Once while lying on his back in the grass behind his home in Fort Scott, Kansas, Gordon Parks heard music. It sounded like a symphony. He sat up to see where the music was coming from. Then he realized that he "heard" the music inside his head. He ran home and tried to play the music on the piano. Gordon knew nothing about musical notes or reading music, but he was able to play the music he heard. He knew right then that his imagination was a powerful thing.

Gordon's mother died when he was 16. Just before she died, she called Gordon to her bedside. "Son," she told him, "never give up trying to do your best." Gordon remembered his mother's advice for the rest of his life. Soon after her death, Gordon was sent to Minnesota to live with his sister. His sister's husband did not like Gordon living there, however, and threw Gordon out of the house. Gordon no longer had a home. He lived in the streets and rode trolley cars all night to stay warm.

For a long time, life was hard for Gordon Parks. At last he found a steady job with the railroad. He

Gordon Parks took this photo of a man sitting on an orange crate in Harlem in 1949.

This photo shows Gordon Parks working at home.

traveled all over the country. Then, in Chicago, Illinois, something important happened. Gordon went to a movie theater and saw some short films made by a famous photographer. He suddenly realized that photographs could be used to tell important and moving stories. The idea changed his life forever. By the time he left the theater, he knew he wanted to become a photographer.

Gordon bought a camera and carried it with him everywhere. At first he took pictures of everything. Then he focused his goal to photographing African Americans living in slum neighborhoods. Gordon yearned to show a side of life that was unknown to most people. He wanted to present this side of life in such a way that it would reach out and touch people's imaginations. Eventually he was hired to take pictures for *Life* magazine. Gordon Parks presented his view of life to all of America, and Americans began to notice.

Later, he became the first African American to make a full-length movie in Hollywood. The movie, called *The Learning Tree,* was based on a book he had written about growing up in Kansas. Gordon Parks was a famous photographer and a first in film history. Through the power of imagination he was able to speak to millions of people.

Middle of America

Geologists tell us that in prehistoric times, parts of Kansas were underneath a huge North American sea. During the last Ice Age, massive ice glaciers traveled over sections of the state. These prehistoric features left behind rich minerals and fertile land. Over thousands of years, this land has been home to many different groups of people. For hundreds of years, it has been home to many generations of farmers.

Today, Kansas is probably as close as any state gets to being typically American. Or it's at least what many people think of as typically American. It is a state where farming, manufacturing, and service industries all carry the economy. It is a place where small towns still survive and the cities are a manageable size. Even the climate is typical—cold winters, hot summers, and moderate springs and autumns. Kansas is also the geographical middle ground of America. In the small Kansas town of Lebanon, a stone monument marks the official center of the contiguous, or connected, United States.

Lebanon, Kansas, is the geographic center of the contiguous United States. The center of the North American continent is also located in Kansas, 40 miles south of Lebanon.

43

The wild sunflower was chosen in 1903 as the official Kansas state flower. The legislature that adopted it wrote that the flower "is full of the life and glory of the past, the pride of the present, and the majesty of the future."

Kansas is certainly well balanced, but no place on Earth can be perfect. The state may have some problems ahead. Many of its farmers are barely getting by, and the aircraft industry is slowing its production. What's more, the state lacks a wide variety of opportunities for its young people. Many of them leave as a result. But Kansans have never been the type of people to sit back and let things happen. Kansas has recorded a steady growth in population since the 1970s. Its efforts in tourism and international trade are broadening the state's economic base for the future. Kansas also has one of the lowest unemployment rates in the nation. Kansas has made it through the slavery battles, the lawless frontier, and the despair of the Dust Bowl—it stands ready for the challenges of the twenty-first century.

Important Historical Events

13,000 B.C.	Paleo-Indians live on the central plains.
A.D. 1000	Native Americans have formed villages and learned to farm.
1541	Francisco Vásquez de Coronado enters the area looking for the Seven Cities of Cíbola. He gives up when he reaches central Kansas.
1682	René-Robert Cavelier, Sieur de La Salle, claims a large part of central North America, including Kansas, for France.
1744	The French build a military and trading post near Leavenworth.
1803	President Thomas Jefferson acquires the Louisiana Purchase, including Kansas, from France.
1804	The Lewis and Clark expedition passes through eastern Kansas.
1806	Zebulon Pike crosses the area.
1819	Stephen H. Long explores the eastern border of present-day Kansas.
1830	Relocation of eastern Native American groups into Kansas begins.
1854	The Kansas Territory is opened to settlement by the Kansas-Nebraska Act.
1855	Proslavery forces take over the Kansas government.
1856	Proslavery forces sack the town of Lawrence. John Brown and his anti-slavery forces fight back.
1861	Kansas is admitted to the Union as a free state in January. The Civil War begins in April.
1862	The Homestead Act is passed.
1863	William Quantrill raids Lawrence, destroying most of the town and killing 150 people.
1867	The Union Pacific Railroad reaches Abilene, and the cattle drives begin. The government fails to provide promised support for Native Americans who relocate to Oklahoma.
1874	The Mennonites bring Turkey Red wheat to Kansas.
1878	The last of the raiding Native Americans in Kansas surrender and leave for Oklahoma.
1887	Susanna Salter, the first woman mayor in the United States, takes office in Argonia.
1890	The first Populist senator is elected to the United States Congress.
1912	Women are given the right to vote in all Kansas elections.
1931	The droughts that lead to the Dust Bowl begin.
1952	Kansas-native Dwight D. Eisenhower is elected President.
1954	Segregated schools are declared unconstitutional by the U.S. Supreme Court in *Brown* v. *Topeka Board of Education*.
1956	The Kansas Turnpike is completed.
1980	Many Kansas farms are lost in a nationwide recession.
1993	Kansas signs a trade agreement with the Leningrad region of Russia.

The Kansas state flag displays the state seal on a field of deep blue. Above the seal is a sunflower, the state flower. The seal shows a farmer plowing, symbolizing Kansas' prosperity as an agricultural state. The 34 stars above the scene represent states. Kansas was the 34th state to join the Union.

Kansas Almanac

Nicknames. Sunflower State, Wheat State, Breadbasket of the World

Capital. Topeka

State Bird. Western meadowlark

State Flower. Sunflower

State Tree. Cottonwood

State Motto. *Ad Astra per Aspera* (To the Stars Through Difficulty)

State Song. "Home on the Range"

State Abbreviations. Kan. (traditional); KS (postal)

Statehood. January 29, 1861, the 34th state

Government. Congress: U.S. senators, 2; U.S. representatives, 4. State Legislature: senators, 40; representatives, 125. Counties: 105

Area. 82,282 sq mi (213,110 sq km), 14th in size among the states

Greatest Distances. north/south, 206 mi (331 km); east/west, 408 mi (656 km)

Elevation. Highest: Mount Sunflower, 4,039 ft (1,231 m). Lowest: 680 ft (207 m)

Population. 1990 Census: 2,485,600 (5% increase over 1980), 32nd among the states. Density: 30 persons per sq mi (12 persons per sq km). Distribution: 69% urban, 31% rural. 1980 Census: 2,364,236

Economy. *Agriculture:* wheat, grain sorghum, corn, soybeans, beef cattle, milk, hogs, sheep, poultry. *Manufacturing:* transportation, especially aircraft, food processing, printed materials. *Mining:* petroleum, natural gas, salt, limestone, coal, helium

State Seal

State Flower: Sunflower

State Bird:
Western meadowlark

Annual Events

★ International Pancake Race in Liberal (February)

★ Kansas Relays in Lawrence (April)

★ Messiah Festival of Music in Lindsborg (April)

★ Flint Hills Rodeo in Strong City (June)

★ Dodge City Days (July)

★ Kickapoo Indian Pow-wow in Horton (July)

★ National Midget Car Races in Belleville (August)

★ Kansas State Fair in Hutchinson (September)

★ Walnut Valley Bluegrass Festival in Winfield (September)

★ Neewollah Festival in Independence (October)

Places to Visit

★ Agricultural Hall of Fame in Bonner Springs

★ Big Brutus Coal Shovel, near West Mineral

★ Dalton Museum in Coffeyville

★ Dodge City Historic Site

★ Dorothy's House in Liberal

★ Eisenhower Center in Abilene

★ Fort Leavenworth, near Leavenworth

★ Geographic Center of the United States in Lebanon

★ John Brown Museum and Memorial Park in Osawatomie

★ Kansas Cosmosphere and Space Center in Hutchinson

★ Kansas Museum of History in Topeka

★ Little House on the Prairie in Independence

★ Mid-America All-Indian Center and Museum in Wichita

Index